The wonder of friends

C. R. Gibson®
FINE GIFTS SINCE 1870

All images © Hulton Getty Picture Collection
Design by Keith Jackson
All text unless otherwise attributed by David and Rebecca Pickering.

Developed by Matthew A. Price, Nashville, Tennessee.

Published by C. R. Gibson®
C. R. Gibson® is a registered trademark of Thomas Nelson, Inc.
Nashville, Tennessee 37214
Printed and bound by L. Rex Printing Company Limited, China

ISBN 0-7667-6159-2
UPC 082272-44980-0
GB4136

The wonder of friends

"You cannot be **friends** upon any other **terms** than upon the **terms of equality**"

– Woodrow Wilson

"Friendship
is in loving
rather than
being loved"

– Robert Bridges

"fun is made to be shared"

"with **friends**, even the **dull** **things** become **exciting**"

"Being accepted, feeling part of a group, I feel great"

"my friends put up with my **bad hair** days"

"friendship is when you look at the world the same way"

"a friend
believes in
your dreams,
even
when big
they are very
and you are
very small"

"With my friends, I can be utterly me. I can tell them how I feel. I know they'll always listen"

"Hold a true friend
with both
your
hands"

– Nigerian Proverb

"a friend is
someone
you really
trust"

"true friendship bridges
every barrier - laughs at every
obstacle"

"fun is doing
almost anything
with people I enjoy"
– David Cunningham

"What is a friend?
A single soul
in two bodies"
– Aristotle